ARTISTIC PLANTS & FLOWERS

Edited by

M. P. Verneuil

Dover Publications, Inc.
Mineola, New York

Copyright

Bibliographical Note

This Dover edition, first published in 2009, is a new selection of 120 plates from *Encyclopédie artistique et documentaire de la plante,* originally published as a four-volume set by the Librairie Centrale des Beaux-Arts, Paris, in 1904–08.

DOVER *Pictorial Archive* SERIES

Library of Congress Cataloging-in-Publication Data

Encyclopédie artistique et documentaire de la plante. Selections.
Artistic plants and flowers / edited by M. P. Verneuil.
p. cm. — (Dover pictorial archive series)
"This Dover edition, first published in 2009, is a new selection of 120 plates from Encyclopédie artistique et documentaire de la plante, originally published as a four-volume set by the Librairie Centrale des Beaux-Arts, Paris, in 1904–08.
ISBN-13: 978-0-486-47251-5
ISBN-10: 0-486-47251-5
1. Decoration and ornament—Plant forms—Pictorial works. I. Verneuil, M. P. (Maurice Pillard), 1869–1942. II. Title.

NK1560.E53 2009
745.4—dc22

2009018129

Manufactured in the United States by Courier Corporation
47251501
www.doverpublications.com

Note

Depicting the exquisite beauty and wide variety of lush flowers and plants in full bloom, the present volume reproduces, in full color, a selection of 120 plates from a rare four-volume French publication originally published in 1904–08. This spectacular work showcases the graceful, sinuous lines of the Art Nouveau style. A leading figure in the Art Nouveau movement, M. P. Verneuil was enthralled with the decorative potential of flowers and floral arrangements, and this collection features elegant renderings of blooms by such popular artists of the early twentieth century as M. Méheut, Alphonse Mucha, and other noted illustrators.

Glorious images of blossoms and flowers have been carefully selected and meticulously reproduced to provide a rich treasury of botanical illustration. An assortment of familiar flowers such as lilacs, roses, dahlias, poppies, and tulips are represented in exceptionally fine detail with realistic, vibrant colors. Contrasted with these gorgeous botanical illustrations are precise and expressive black-and-white renderings of the same flower. These illustrations are arranged in alphabetical order by the common name of each flower.

List of Plates

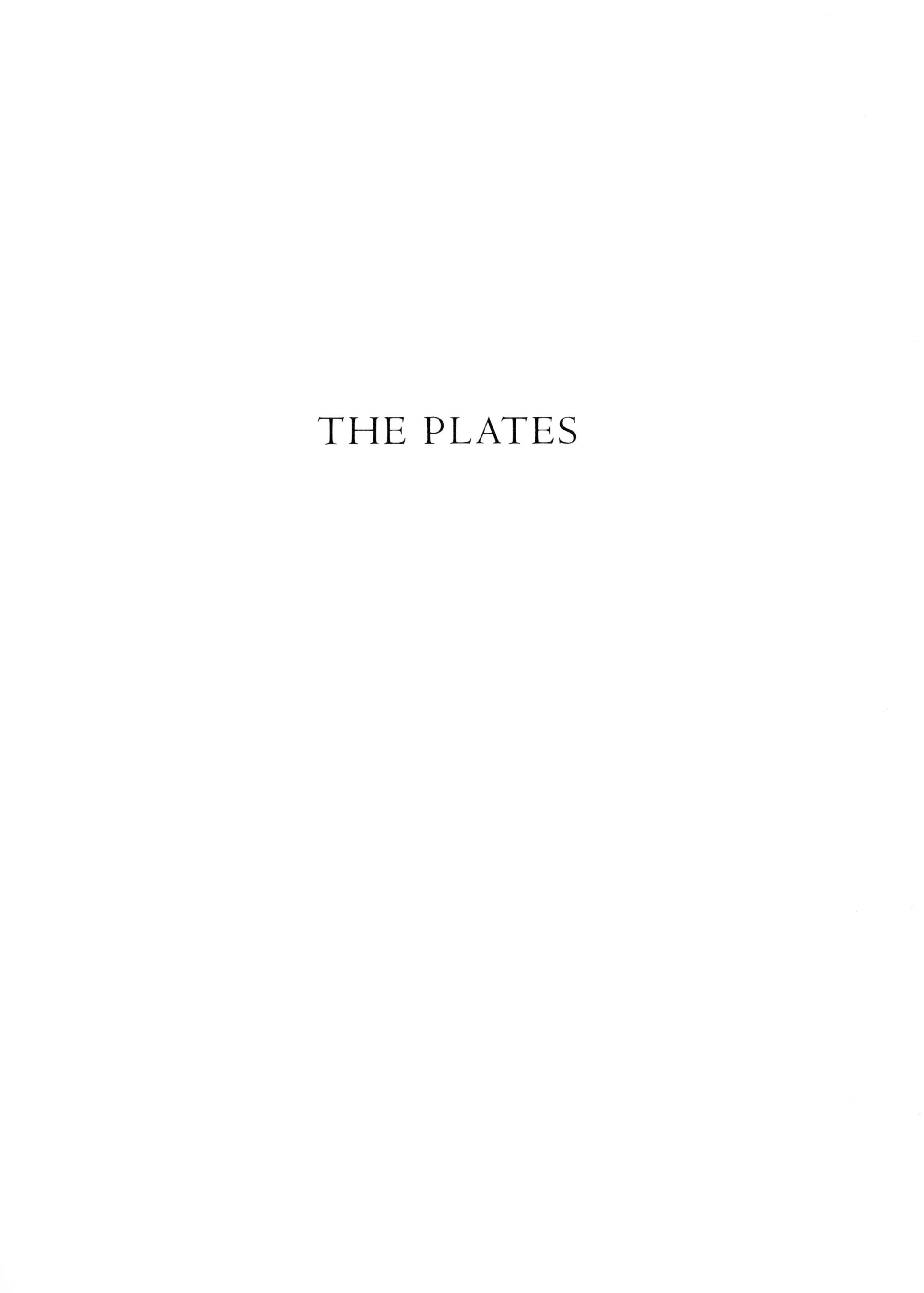

THE PLATES

2 Anemone

A Bailly.

4 Anthurium

GROUPE DE BOUTONS

8 Aster

Aster

 Azalea

L Fuchs

12 Begonia

h. BELLERY DESFONTAINES

16 Blackberry

Jeunes
Pousses.

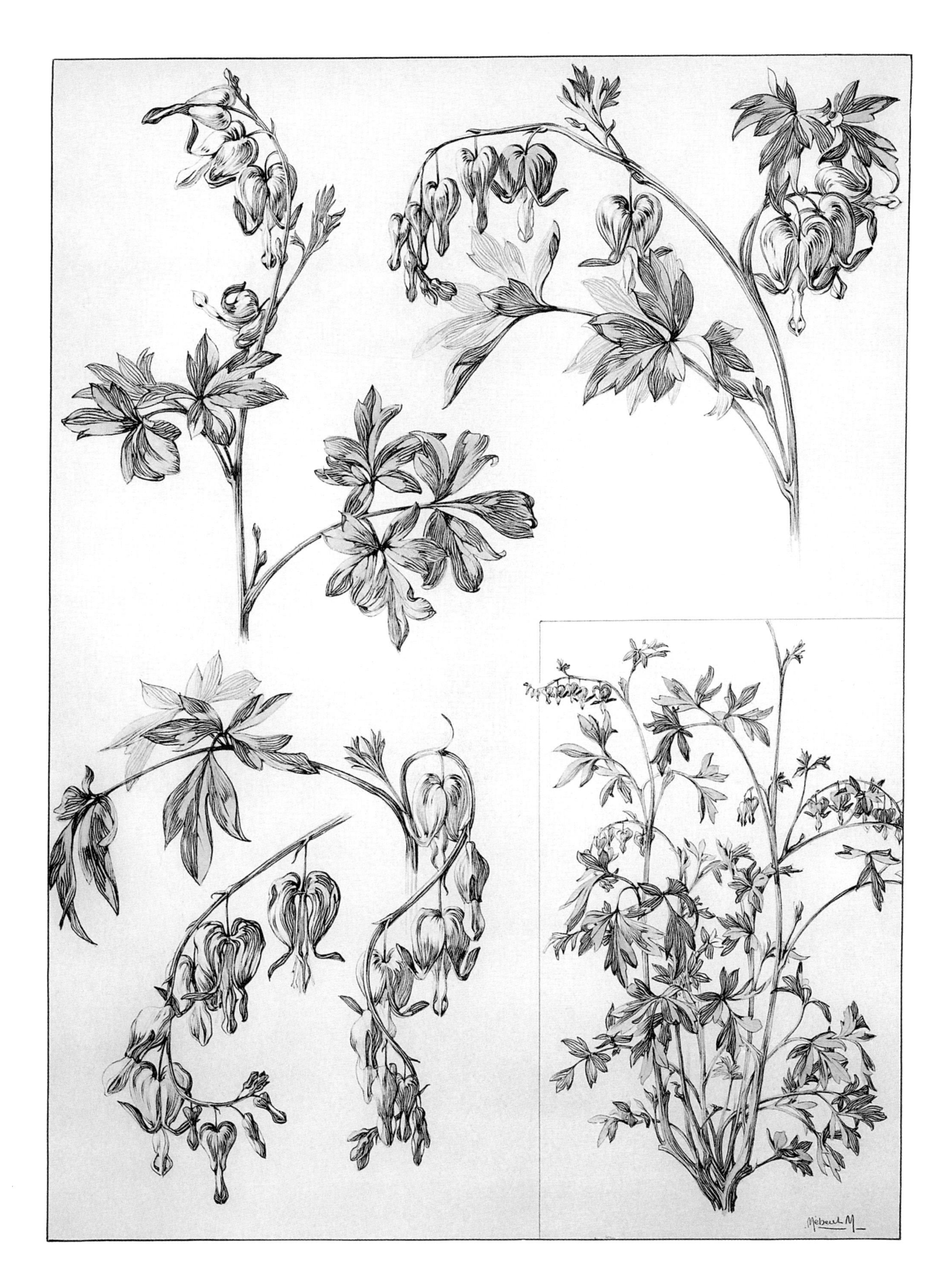

18 Bleeding heart

Bleeding heart

20 Cactus

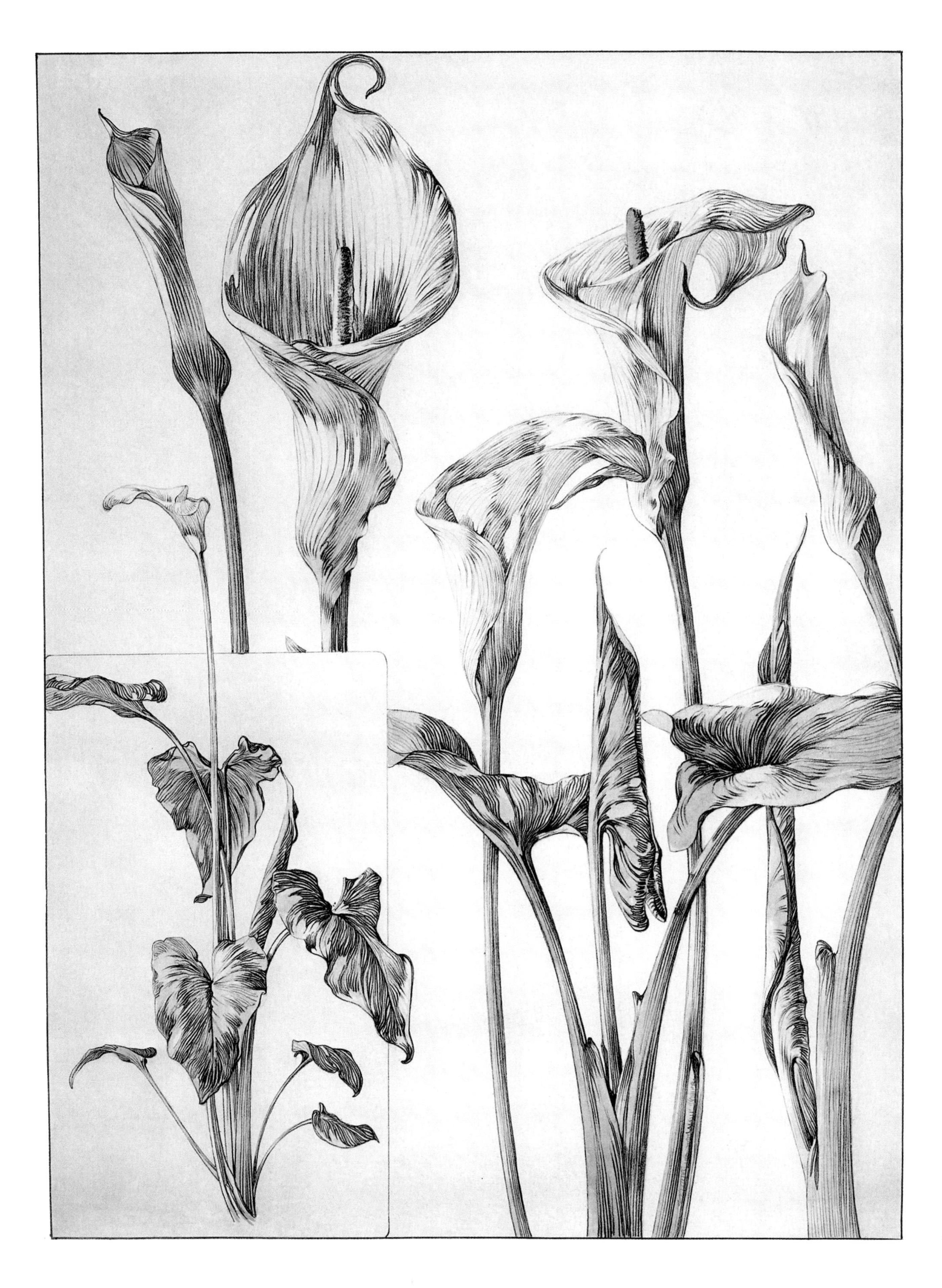

 Calla lily

Calla lily

 Chamomile

Mehut M.

 Cherry

A Bailly

32 China aster

34 Chrysanthemum

Chrysanthemum

36 Clematis

38 Columbine

40 Congo lily

Congo lily

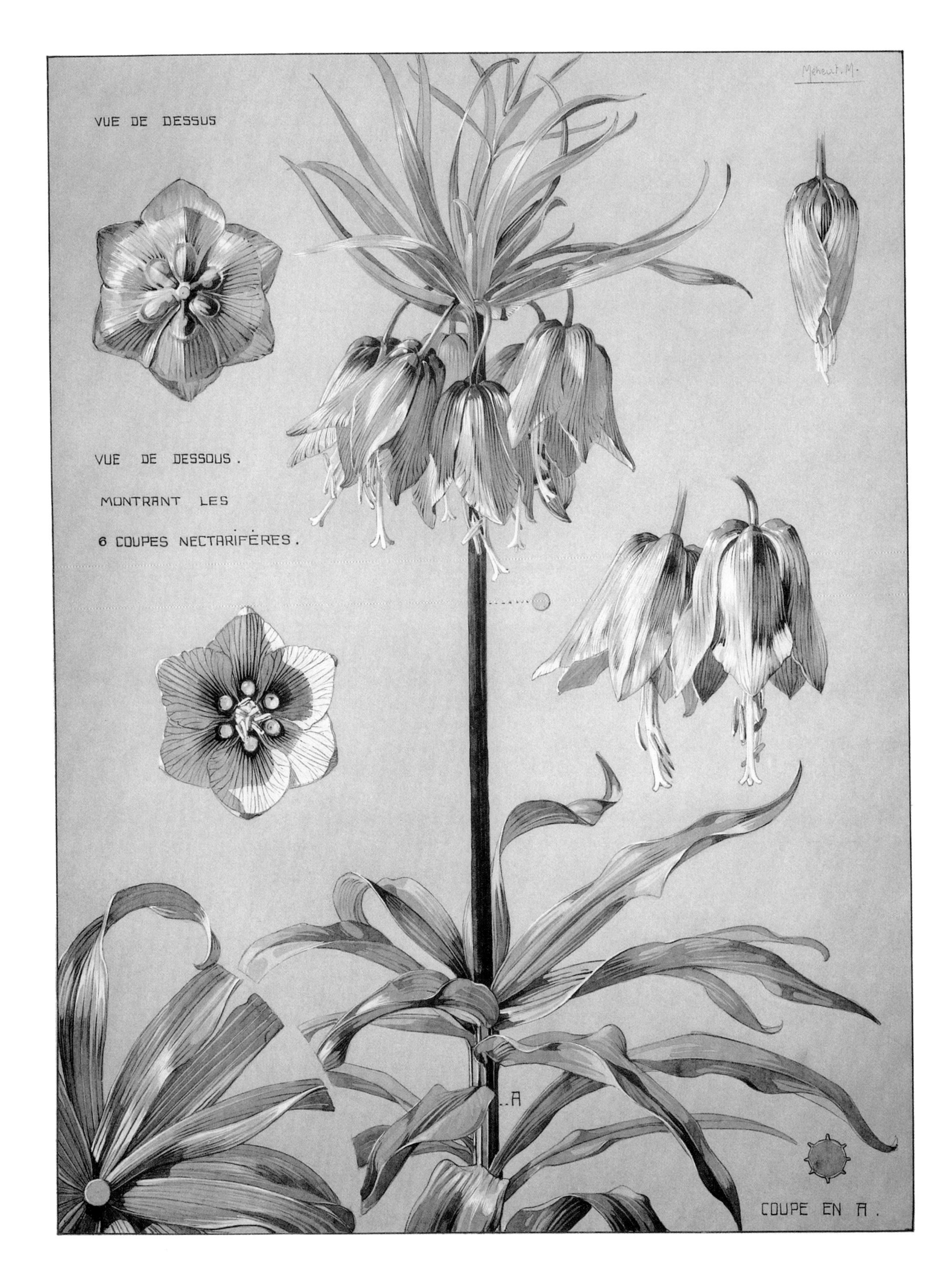

 Crown imperial

Crown imperial

44 Cypripedium orchid

Cypripedium orchid

48 Dandelion

 Foxglove

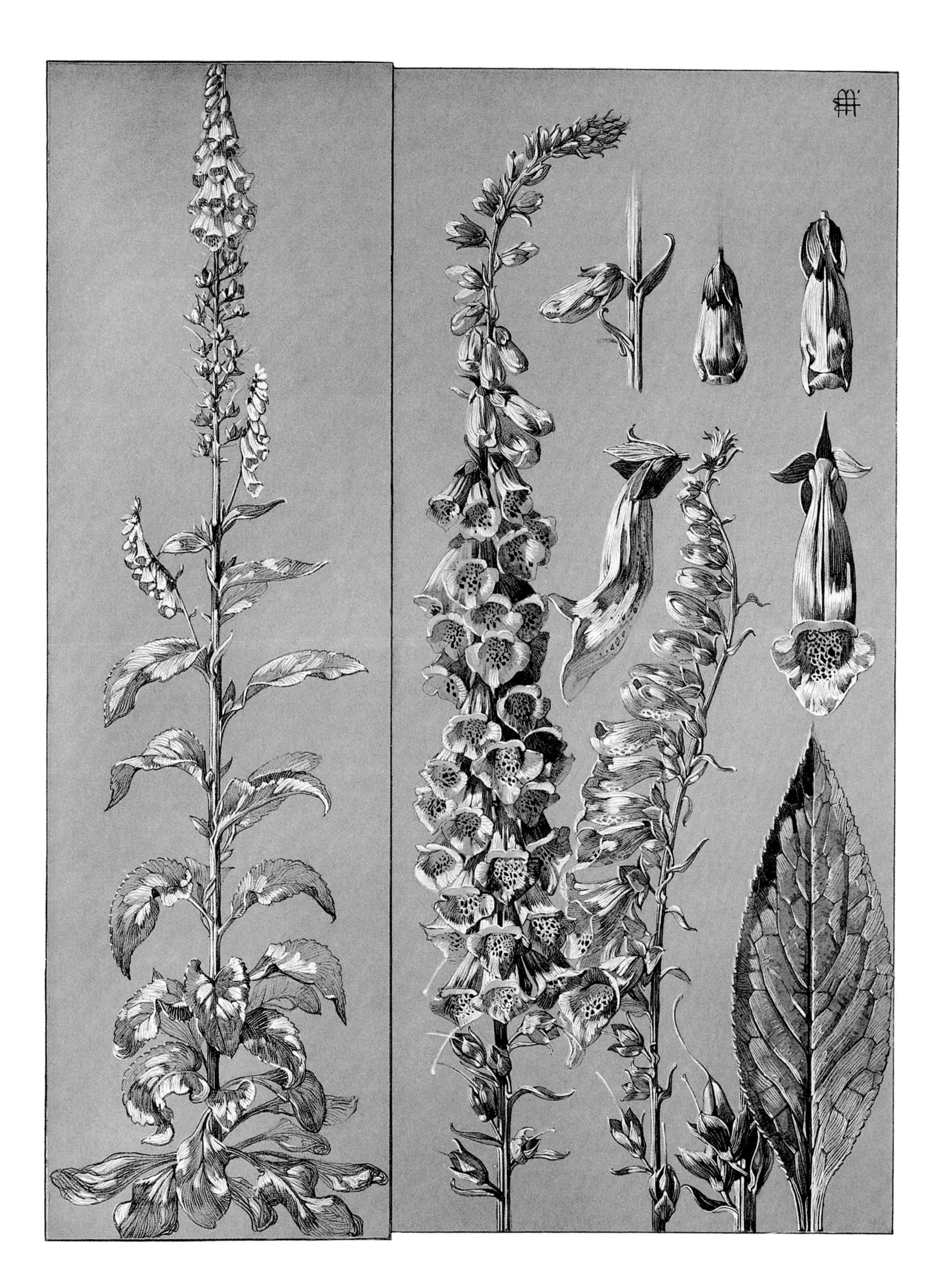

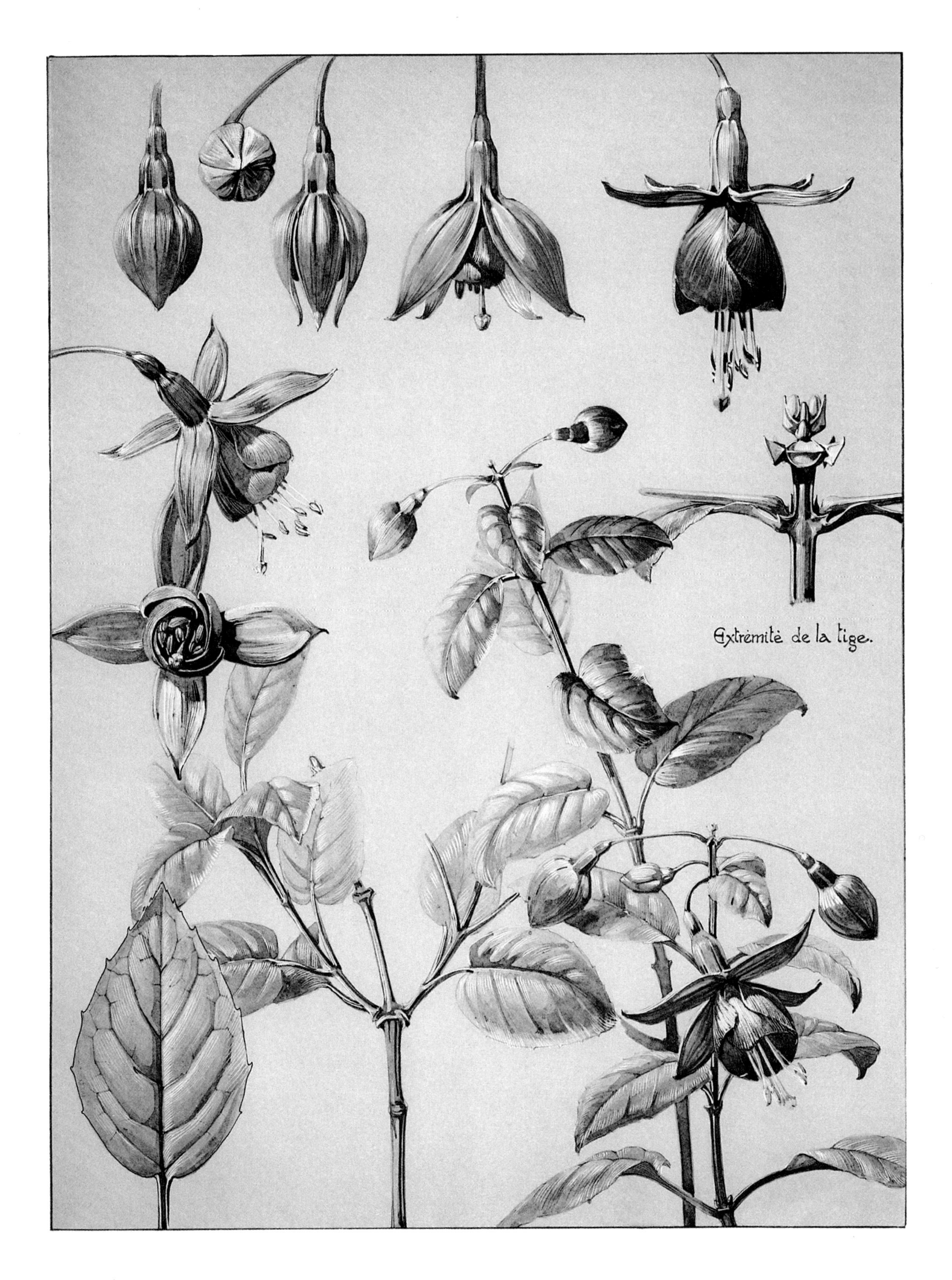
Extrémité de la tige.

A. Bailly

56 Geranium

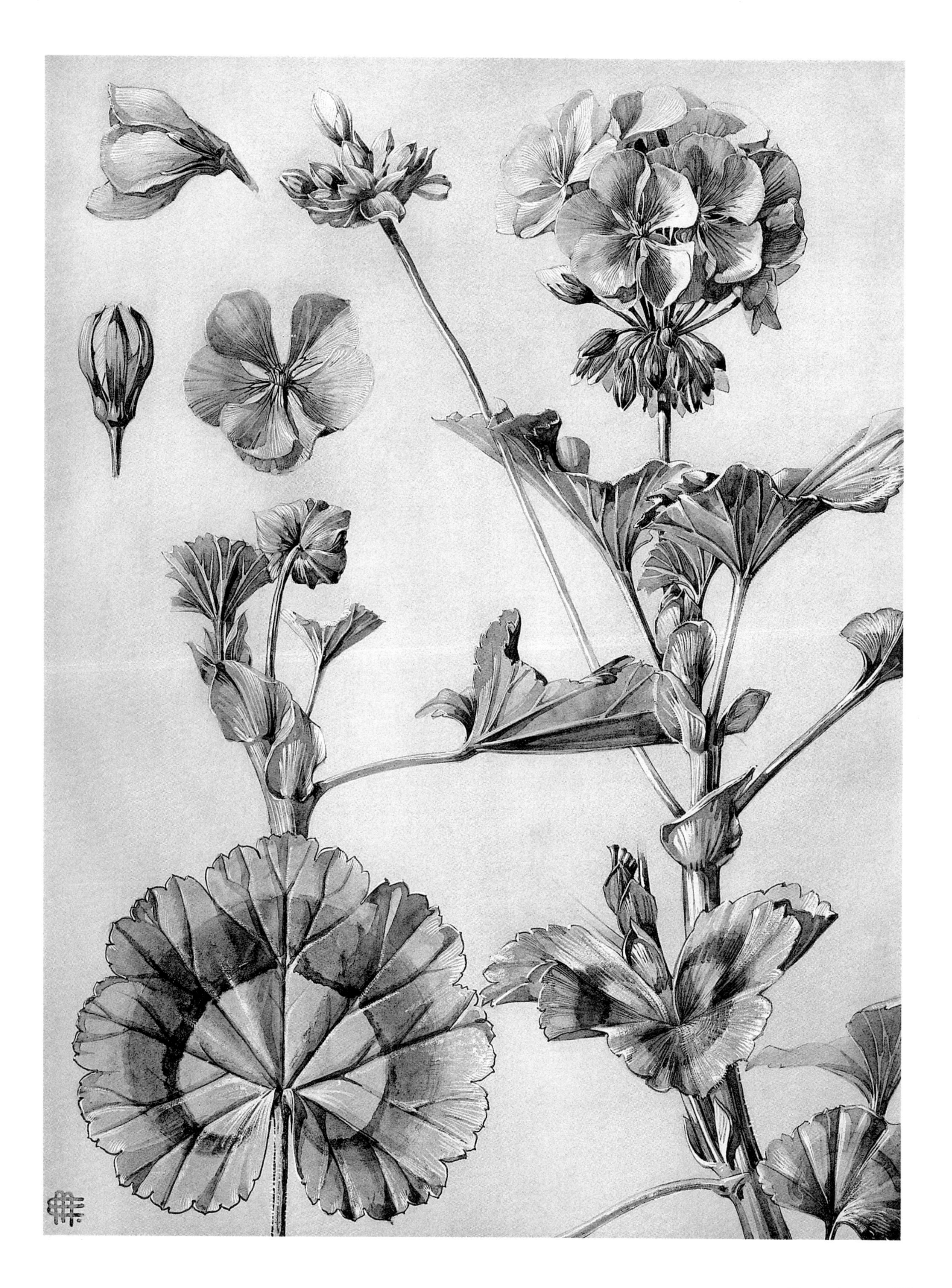

Geranium

58 Gladiolus

Gladiolus

:FLEURS:

62 Hazel

Hazel

64 Horse chestnut

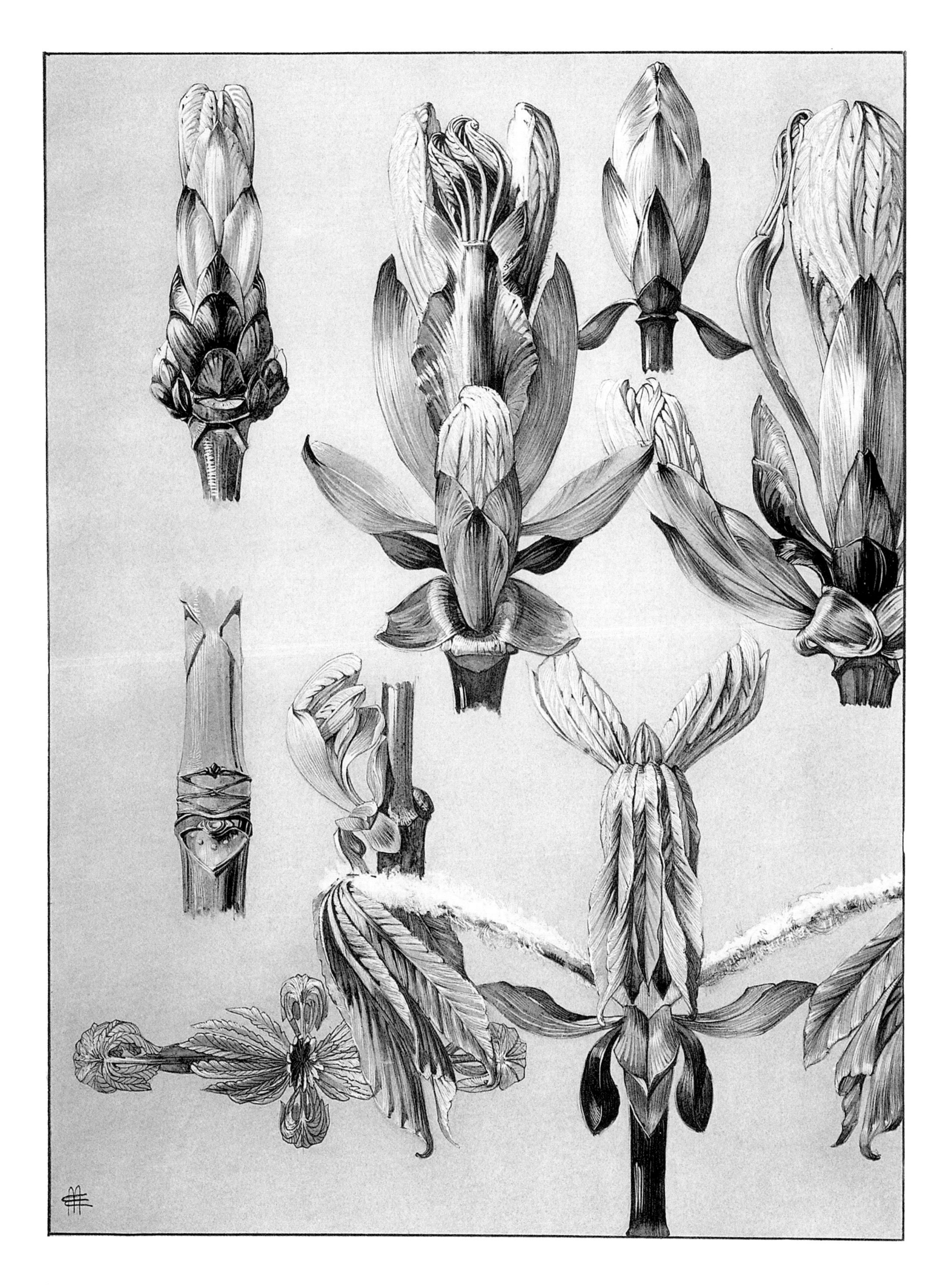

 Ivy

A. Bailly.

 Lilac

74 Lily of the valley

Lily of the valley

78 Mimosa

80 Nasturtium

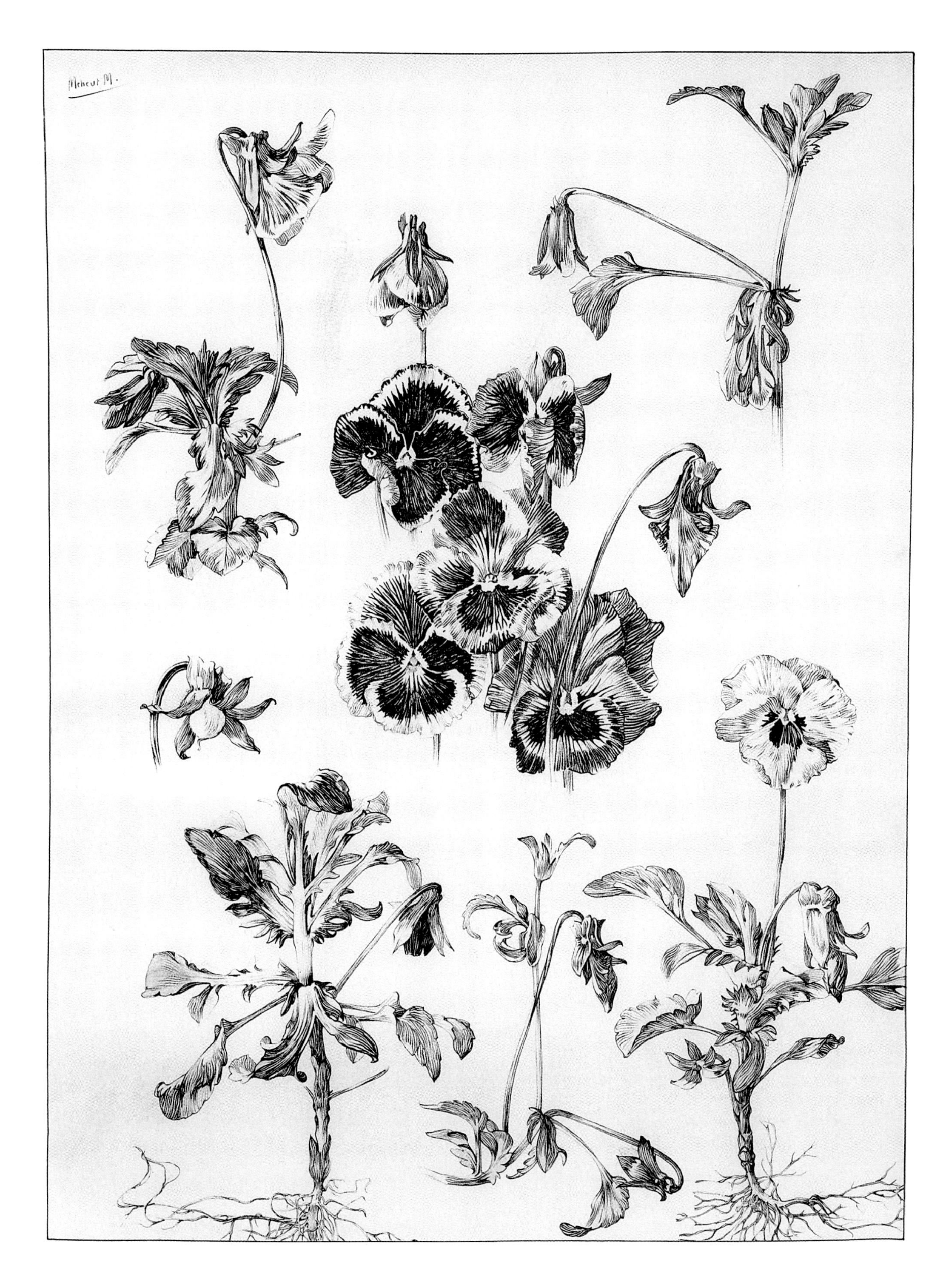

 Pansy

Pansy

84 Passion flower

A.B

90 Petunia

Petunia

 Phlox

 Poppy

96 Potato

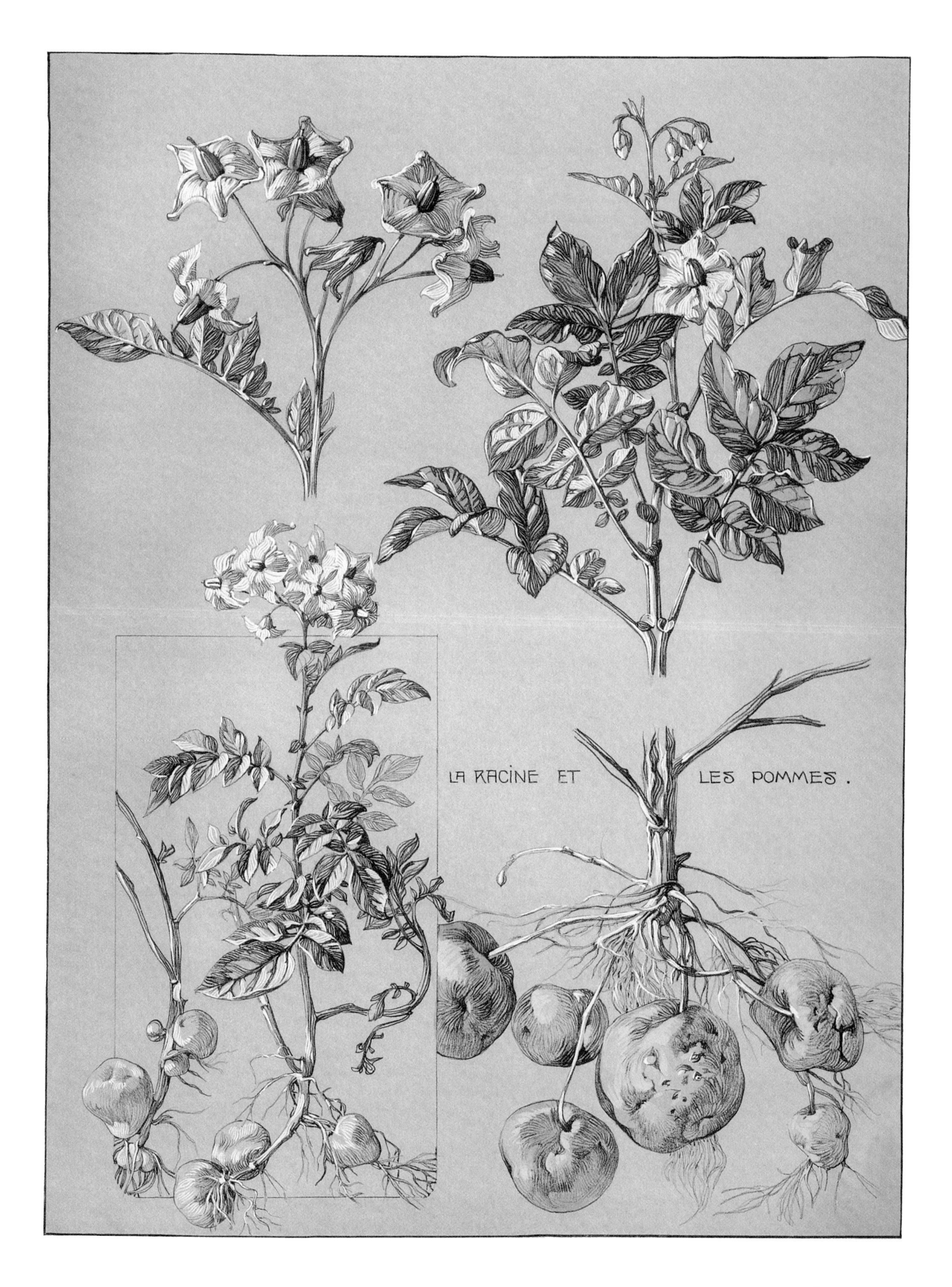
LA RACINE ET LES POMMES .

98 Rhododendron

Rhododendron

 Rose

Snapdragon

104 Snowball or guelder-rose

Snowball or guelder-rose

.Coupe de la tige en A.
.... Feuille
A

Sunflower

108 Sweet pea

 Sweet William

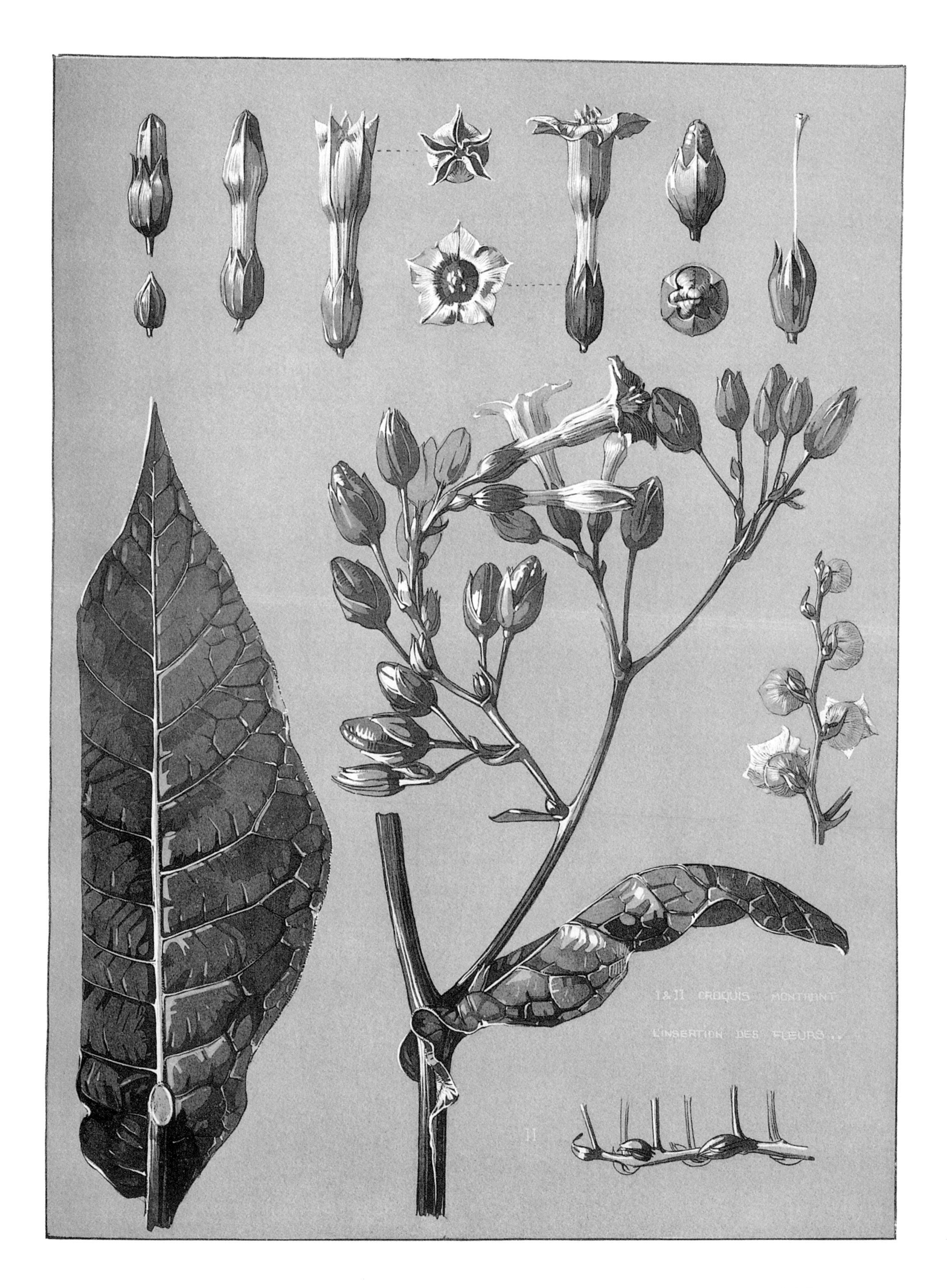
I & II CROQUIS MONTRANT
L'INSERTION DES FLEURS..
II

114 Tomato

Tomato

116 Trumpet creeper

Trumpet creeper

120 Violet